THE MONK'S

Poetry by James Harpur

A VISION OF COMETS

James Harpur

THE MONK'S DREAM

with best wishes,
James Harpur

ANVIL PRESS POETRY

Published in 1996
by Anvil Press Poetry Ltd
Neptune House 70 Royal Hill London SE10 8RT

Copyright © James Harpur 1996

This book is published with financial assistance from
The Arts Council of England

ISBN 0 85646 278 0

A catalogue record for this book
is available from the British Library

The author's rights have been asserted in accordance with
the Copyright, Designs and Patents Act 1988

All rights reserved

Set in Bembo by Anvil
Printed and bound in England
by Morganprint (Blackheath) Ltd
Distributed by Password, Manchester

TO MERRILY, PATRICK AND JOHN
AND IN MEMORY OF MY MOTHER AND FATHER

ACKNOWLEDGEMENTS

The author would like to thank Eveline O'Donovan and Anna Adams for their help and encouragement. The poem 'Gilgamesh and the Death of Enkidu' was based on translations of and commentaries on *The Epic of Gilgamesh*, including: Stephanie Dalley, *Myths from Mesopotamia* (1989); Henri Frankfort *et al.*, *Before Philosophy* (1949); Thorkild Jacobsen, *The Treasures of Darkness* (1976); and N. K. Sandars, *The Epic of Gilgamesh* (1964).

Poems in this collection have previously been published in the following publications: *Acumen*, *Agenda*, the *Independent*, *Poetry Ireland Review*, *Poetry Review*, *Poetry Wales*, the *Spectator*, the *Swansea Review*.

'The Frame of Furnace Light' is an extended version of the poem that won the Poetry Society's National Poetry Competition, 1995.

'Two Big Games' was broadcast on *Poetry Please!* (BBC Radio 4)

'Rugby Union' was awarded third prize in the Norwich Writers Open Poetry Competition 1994.

'Memorial Service' won third prize in the Barnet Open Poetry Competition 1994 and was broadcast on Channel 4 Ceefax.

'The Young Man of Galway's Lament' won third prize in the 1994 Yorkshire Open Poetry Competition.

The author gratefully acknowledges the Arts Council of England for a writer's bursary in 1996.

NOTE: an asterisk in the text at the foot or head of a page indicates a stanza or section break.

CONTENTS

The Flight of the Sparrow	9
The Apparition	10
The Paestum Diver	12
My Mother's Gardener	13
David Inshaw's *Owl and Chestnut Tree*	14
Creüsa's Ghost	15
The Monk's Dream	17

THE FRAME OF FURNACE LIGHT

Coming Home	21
My Father's Flat	22
Two Big Games	23
Rugby Union	24
Visiting	25
Intensive Care	26
The Return	27
Last Visit	28
Coma	29
Death	30
Corn Circle	31
Cremation	32
Naming of Parts	33
Memorial Service	34
Last Rites	35

Gilgamesh and the Death of Enkidu	37
Lazarus	43
The Road to Westport	51
The Young Man of Galway's Lament	58

The Flight of the Sparrow

'My lord, although we cannot know
The mysteries of the afterlife
The span of time we spend on earth
Appears to me to be like this:
Imagine sitting in your hall
In winter, feasting with your chiefs
And counsellors – your faces glowing
From flames that crackle in the hearth.
Outside, the wintry night is lashed
By winds and driving rain and snow.
Suddenly a sparrow darts in
Through a door, flits across the hall
And flies out through another one.
Inside, cocooned in light and warmth
It can enjoy a moment's calm
Before it vanishes, rejoining
The freezing night from which it came.

Such is our journey through this life.
But as to what's in store for us
Beyond the doors of birth and death
We are completely in the dark.'

from Bede: *A History of the English Church and People*, 11:13

The Apparition

In autumn evening light
Withdrawing from our valley
Apocalyptic clouds

Were rolling slowly onward
Like a dark armada
Of bloated zeppelins.

Then from out of nowhere
Above the static ridge
A hanging sphere appeared

And floated like a phantom
Over hilltop houses
And the nagging of a dog.

The rounded silhouette pursued
A horizontal course
Conferred pure silence

Until a rasp of fire
Hollowed out its volume
With crinkling flaming light

So that for an instant
Through its muted canvas
The globe became a sun

Before its orange core
Shrivelled to its source
To merge with the clouds.

The buoyant sphere sailed on
Its gorgeous solar blaze
Rising, dying, rising...

Then it slipped across the hills
To light the darkening folds
Of the valley just beyond.

The Paestum Diver

Paint this stone sarcophagus
With scenes of my funeral feast.
Gather my old companions
And place them on soft couches.

Release their tongues with wine
Caress the flesh of their ephebes
Canoodle tunes from flutes
Pluck harmonics from the lyres.

I have left it all behind me.
My tongue is scummed with wine
Music shrills the silence
And skin on skin sickens.

Paint the colours rich and true.
Let sensuality stain
This cool ascetic tomb –
Except the inside of the lid:

Here show the boundless ocean
A tree or two with fernlike branches
The framework of a diving board;
Keep it delicate and simple.

And show me stripped to nothing
A naked shining soul in flight
Diving through my sensate life
To the waters of oblivion.

My Mother's Gardener

For some weeks absent, he tinkered at the lock
Sprang open the rickety lichened gate
And shuffled boggle-eyed as if in shock
Across the unkempt lawn he used to cut.

His blacksmith's frame fell forward in a stoop
A heavy coat drew down his wasted muscles
His thickset face had been reduced like soap
His skin was barely lit by red corpuscles.

He told us all about his blood transfusion
Explained he could not garden any longer.
As he left, the bolted grass he stepped on
Rose quietly in the wake of his departure.

David Inshaw's
Owl and Chestnut Tree

The snuffed candles of the chestnut gently fume,
The shadow of its girth a pool of darkness

Behind, wraith-swirled like Lake Tartarus
Fields and hedges fade inside the fading light

The moon's fullness ascends above the landscape
Smoke cleansed white by fire drifts upward

An owl has come back early from its masked ball
Its lunar face is plunged with two black seas:

I am the sentinel of the land you see before you.
This world is lit only by your thoughts.

To enter you must leave behind your gross accumulations.
Awake from sleep and cross the threshold.

Creüsa's Ghost

Troy's treasures, snatched from burning shrines,
Altars, bowls of solid gold and stolen garments
Were piled in heaps from all around the city.
Children and trembling women stretched out in a line.
Despite the risk I yelled into the darkness
And my shouts ricochetted along the streets.
Dispirited I called again and again
For Creüsa but my cries were not returned.
Then as I madly searched in every house
The mournful ghost – the shade of Creüsa –
Loomed larger than in life before my eyes.
Stunned, struck dumb, I felt my hackles rise.
Then to allay my fears she spoke these words:

'Dear husband, what use is your demented grief?
The gods have willed the course of these events.
You are forbidden to take me on your voyage –
The lord of high Olympus does not permit it.
For you a lengthy exile is in store:
Your ships must plough a vast expanse of sea
Until you reach Hesperia, the land of the west,
Where through the fertile fields of farmers
The Lydian Tiber flows in gentle curves.
There a kingdom and a royal wife await you
And you will enjoy days of happiness.
Do not shed tears for your beloved Creüsa.
I am a Trojan and the wife of Venus's son –
I will not see the oppressive mansions
Of the Myrmidons and Dolopians.
Nor will I become some Greek woman's slave.

The great mother of the gods will keep me here.
And now, fare well – save your love for our child.'

With this she left me weeping, bursting to speak
Yet tongue-tied, and melted into thin air.
Three times I tried to throw my arms around her neck:
Three times her ghostly form escaped my grasping hands
As if she were a breeze, or just a fading dream.

Aeneid II: 763–94

The Monk's Dream

*'He is a monk, and dreams for money like a monk;
give him a hundred shillings.'*
                    WILLIAM II, AS REPORTED BY
                    WILLIAM OF MALMESBURY

*'What reaches you could not possibly have missed you,
and what misses you could not possibly have reached you.'*
                    TRADITIONAL ARAB SAYING

That August dawn, the fields star-dewed with light,
A foreign monk – he never said his name –
Came to tell me of his dream the previous night
Insisting I should tell it to King William.

Oozing maleficence, the king had burst
Into a church intent on sacrilege:
Seizing a wooden crucifix he first
Gnawed its outstretched arms then bit its bolted legs

When suddenly the goaded Christ kicked out
And floored the king; as he lay prostrate, his jaws
Opened like the pit of hell and a spout
Of fire, streaking up to heaven, smoked the stars.

When I told my lord, he sneered and blurted
That the night before he too had had a dream:
His blood was being let when up it spurted
Until it dimmed the sun with its frothy stream.

Later, testing God, the king went off to hunt.
The sun, a mad red eye, was in decline
Slanting blue shadows from every branch and trunk
And Walter Tyrell, William's sole companion.

Staring in the bracken-fretted glade for deer
The king, his bow arm at the ready, waited.
Then through the twitching copse a stag appeared:
He aimed, fired and grazed the beast, which fled.

Straightaway Walter saw another one
And loosed an arrow... then held his breath
As it pierced the body of our sovereign,
Who plunged down on the shaft to hasten death.

I, Robert Fitz Hamon, leave this record
Of the day's events as I was told them.
I later heard that Walter fled abroad
And the foreign monk was never seen again.

But I often wonder if his dream
Could have altered William's destiny –
Are we constricted to a star-fixed scheme
Or can we execute our actions freely?

This I do know: we must cleanse our lives of blood
Do penance for transgressions of the past
Pray for our souls and make our peace with God
And live each day as if it were the last:

For who knows when the arrow gripped by fate
In muscled tension, quivering for the kill
On an ignored or unknown future date,
Will send us into paradise, or hell.

THE FRAME
OF FURNACE LIGHT

Each of us finds the world of death fitted to himself.
Aeneid VI: 743

Coming Home

We thought the start seemed quite innocuous:
A phone call – *just a routine operation*;
A grumbling gall bladder, nothing to shock us.

But for him this was the start of a voyage
Into a pre-war life, a transformation
Begun by scalpel, needles, drips and drugs.

In time, bound to his bed, he became softer,
More serene, as the bluster leaked with each gasp
Extracted by the ventilator.

And as Odysseus' hound divined the beggar
We saw him suddenly step out from the past
And welcomed home this long-returning stranger:

The father who planted trees for football posts;
The wandering husband who'd left behind a ghost.

My Father's Flat

Tugging apart the curtains every day
He always saw, three stories up, a grand
Sweep of the Thames, the trees of Battersea

And, squatting there, the Japanese pagoda –
Inflaming – a parody of a bandstand,
Its four sides flaunting a golden Buddha.

It glowed like a lantern near the glitzy braid
Of Albert Bridge at night.
                       If he had crossed
The river he might have heard *Renounce the world*

Escape the gilded lips or seen Gautama lying
In mortal sleep, his face relaxed, his flesh released;
Even in death, teaching the art of dying.

At night, across the river two golden eyes burn
Into the heavy velvet of the curtain.

Two Big Games

My first soccer match was like a waking dream.
Floodlights as pure as moons arc-lit the grass,
The white lines and royal colours of the teams.

Tobacco smoke cloaked the roars and sucked-in hush
Like sea mist. My father, in the aftermath,
Cursed the crowd, bracing to save me from the crush.

Years later at our first big rugby match
I was lost in impassioned ecstasy
Until the final whistle when I watched

His jittery legs heave up his wheezing frame;
I followed close as he picked his way
Down the stairs and pretended not to shield him

From the thickening wedge of bodies and to hide
The stone-faced feelings jostling me inside.

Rugby Union

Magicked inside a sunlit television
We sit apart, my father flushed and shrunken
Gulping air, both entranced by Rugby Union:

The cancelling man-for-man polarities
The chaos turning to organic patterns
Bodies converging on the ball like bees

Braced deadlocks of the scrum, the popped release
Of tension – the ball flung along a line
As ordered as a wheeling skein of geese.

Gradually the years of absence tick away
And in the silence we are locked as one
Gripped by the infectious currents of the play:

His body flows with my adrenalin
My lungs are shortened by his fevered breathing.

Visiting

It could be the departure lounge at Athens:
Sound-proof glass, anxious Arabs, Greeks, swept marble.
Only the deep lifts hint at any menace.

Within the silent maze of corridors
My mind winds up as I close in on my goal
Dry-mouthed like Theseus sensing the Minotaur.

Room 303 – there he is! Half man, half bed,
Bellowing with laughter, his blubbery belly
Quivering above the sheets, his twitchy head

Ablaze with pre-op nerves and quickfire jokes,
A bull tycoon as helpless as a puppy
Eager for pats and reassuring strokes.

At length I leave. My unravelled mind is led
From trail to trail, but cannot keep the thread.

Intensive Care

A realm of coming back and passing over,
It lies below the ground behind sealed doors.
I give the password, cross the threshold, enter

And see moving tableaux from a scene in hell:
Robed psychopomps and flickering monitors
Masked neophytes equipped with charts and needles

A line of slabs adorned with naked creatures
Collapsed like boneless chickens and restrained
By wires, their stomachs laddered black in stitches.

I sit beside my specimen, who lies
With punctured throat and softly sagging head
And hope that when at last he lifts his eyes

He sees the bleared face of his youngest son,
Not the impatient bristling brows of Charon.

The Return

Anaesthetized, he purrs with measured doses
Of ventilated air, an artificial spirit
Which gently animates his vacant carcass

Until he suddenly comes round, blinks madly,
Feels tubing at his throat and in panic
Mimes for paper, pen, and scrawls 'Where am I?'

You who were floating in the depths of space,
Weightless, revolving slowly, who saw the stars
Drifting into distant ribboned galaxies

Yet prickling your skin like phosphorescent atoms
And heard the spinning music of the spheres
Crisscrossing like whales' eerie ocean hymns –

You have landed safely on the planet earth;
Behold your shrunken bed, your universe.

Last Visit

A Friday evening in the year of drought.
The open window flicked with flying insects
The room was soft with balmy air and light.

My ailing father plumped in bed seemed carefree
As if a long-term deadline had been met.
Relaxed, we chatted, idly watched TV...

If I had known it was to be our last time
At what moment could I have departed,
Ever adding seconds of his life to mine?

As it was I picked a random pause to go,
As usual kissed the scar on his bald head
And with a 'see you soon' stepped out into

The lamplight of the slow embalming summer
Which seemed as if it would last forever.

Coma

My father sits up slumped inside a coma;
His face nodding slowly on his neck, fed
By the soft pushings of the ventilator.

Instructed that he may not last the night,
I lie down keeping vigil by his bed
Alarmed in the gangrenous demi-light

By his hobgoblin mask, his loosened mouth
Agape, disgorging darkness like a gargoyle;
And still his head rocks slowly back and forth.

All is quiet except the hushing breath
Of the ventilator. Tense, cramped, I recoil
From sleep in case it somehow brings on death

Until I gently drift away like James in the
Darkness of the garden of Gethsemane.

Death

His plump familiar body sits in bed;
We watch his slackened face, unwaking eyes
And black fanged mouth, its lower jaw unhinged.

His head nods gently with the ventilator;
A doctor comes to probe his dying pulse
And coolly notes his fingertips are bluer.

Brain-dead, he may have passed away already
While we attend a grisly simulacrum –
A clockwork puppet, a ghost-train effigy.

And so it goes on till a specialist
Discreet, soft-spoken, leads us from the room:
We wait, and know the cycle is accomplished.

I slip in again to view his body
And see a stranger: Death looks up at me.

Corn Circle

It was the third day after he was dead,
His body yet to be consigned to fire.
We were marooned in limbo, as becalmed

As the endless days of summer rolling by,
Turning to ash the surface soils of Wiltshire
And shrinking the chalk streams of our valley.

That evening we stood on Pepperbox Hill
Gazing at fields embalmed in golden heat
And there, as if cut from the corn, a circle.

We walked down and picked our way through rows
Towards the solar disc burning in the wheat
And crossed the threshold of the temenos

Entering the benediction of the stasis
The heart of the sun, whirling, motionless.

Cremation

The hearse sharks through the shoals of Putney
Homing towards the bloodless drive-in chapel,
Bearing our father on his final journey.

A scattering of family, friends, we try
To sing to life this nuclear funeral.
The unknown vicar speaks... we kneel to pray

And watch the climax of the rite of passage:
The coffin sliding into the furnace
With the panache of airport reclaim baggage.

Outside, as yet more mourners wait, we return
To sanguine selves, taking home the ashes
Of all he was within a plastic urn,

Numbing out the absence, the ritual vacuum,
The last *reductio ad absurdum*.

Naming of Parts

The lungs that sucked the foaming Irish Sea
The tongue that sprung its traps of wit and puns
The nails that plucked the twinkling ukelele

The feet that trod the mud towards the Po
The hands that fed the water-cooled machine guns
The ears that heard the silence at Cassino

The freckled scalp that gashed a stalactite
The arm that kept a tennis rally going
The eyes that saw the comet burn the night

Have duly carried out their mortal service
And free from tyranny of endless doing
Have come to rest in blissfulness of peace

As dead appendages of coffined flesh
The gorgeous flames will turn to fiery ash.

Memorial Service

Although the images dim, my mind recalls
A sharpened turquoise morning in September,
The sun burning Blackfriars and St Paul's

And people ghosting into church – the cast
Of his life, each a living tessera,
A tiny embered memory of his past

And, unforgettable, Fauré's *Requiem*,
Abide with Me, *Swing Low Sweet Chariot*,
The burnished echoes of *Jerusalem*.

Afterwards, friends and cronies from his club
Flowed out through the frame of furnace light
And brother soldiers slipped off to the pub

To blink at gun-flash memories of the Po,
To blank out who would be the next to go.

Last Rites

A coastguard pilot in his spotter plane
Took off towards the tight-lipped sky above
Bearing the urn of carbon flesh and bone.

Clouds softened and with a gradual smile the sun
Caressed the humming craft into a dove
Winging its shadow to the flecked horizon.

Unseen the dusty atoms drifted down,
Acquiesced on the surface of the sea
Completing the final dissolution.

Now beady darting fish invade his grave.
His tombstone is every ship that passes by.
Nothing remains but litanies of wave on wave

Rushing over gravelly shores where they release
Their hushed prayers, rest in peace, in peace, in peace...

Gilgamesh and the Death of Enkidu

'Dear brother, last night a dream again expanded
In my skull and blew pictures through my eyes.
I stood alone within a stony desert,
The stretched horizons hazed with sallow light
Bathing shadows uniformly from the rocks.
At first there was a breathing, as of wind,
But there was no wind, and the breathing
Caressed my face with soft malignity.
I felt a presence move in unseen towards me
The air grew ranker, the breathing harsher
My lungs were tightened, my hackles prickled
Then flapping like a crazed shadow
A ragged black thing twisted down above me;
Clenching my shoulders with its talons
It pulled its knuckle beak and fumey breath
Into the paralysed fullness of my face
And wrapped my body with its moth-soft wings
Stroked my arms until they lost their nerves
And dangled uselessly like bits of rope.

The creature poked its beak inside my ear
And purred:"Enkidu, your time has come,
I am all you have neglected and destroyed,
Your bestial life tricked from you by the whore,
The indecisions that stuttered in your head
The semi-truths that weaved their half-deceits
The drunken words that pleased your wine-smug lips
I am the bull of heaven you butchered
Humbaba, whom you slaughtered in the forest,
The cedar trees whose soaring spines you severed

I am the oceanic darkness of your sleep
Through which your dreams swim on like coloured fish.
I have come to take you to the underworld
To Queen Irkalla's palace of the dead
From which no mortal has returned."'

Gilgamesh watched his friend, his brother,
His yellow skin racked across his cheekbones
His eyes as dry and black as scarab beetles
His brown lips cracked apart like crusts of bread.
And he dammed the spate of grief that rushed
Upward from his heart towards his throat.

'The creature led me to the house of death
And there within the muffled darkness I saw
The souls of the deceased disguised as birds.
They stretched black wings like gaping yawns
Then shifted, stirring dust as fine as funeral ash.
As I followed round the snuffling silhouettes
I recognized dead kings and princes:
Etana, king of Kish, the king of Ur,
The kings of Shurrupak and Lagash.
Their golden crowns, trimmed beards and pleated robes
Were now charcoal rags and scrags of hair
As they hopped and scuttled with platters of meat
And skins of water for the lords of darkness.'

Gilgamesh, king of Uruk, did not speak.
His brother's dream had drawn him in
And death was creeping snakelike up his spine.

'Beyond the scrabbly traffic of shuffling souls
The gods, impassive, still, sat on their thrones.
There was Samuqan, the god of cattle,

Irkalla, queen of the underworld,
And squatting down before her, Belit-Sheri
Scribbled in her book of death the names of souls.
As if alerted by my trancelike gaze
Her eyes curled up, locked on me, and she spoke:
"Who is he? Who brought him here? Who is he?
Who brought him here? Who is he? Who brought him?"'

'I woke, my lips still fingering her words
Sweat had sluiced the hair across my forehead
And streams of life had shrunk from my body
Like water channels burnt up by the sun.'

Gilgamesh watched his friend, his brother,
Subsiding like a fish on blistered earth,
His robe flung from his naked salt-slicked skin.
He flicked a tear as if it were a fly,
Cleared his throat and with an even voice he said:
'Never in Uruk have I heard a dream like this.
The gods created Irkalla's house of dust
Within your head to show you what lies in wait
After death has seized us like a bailiff.
Bite your fear. You must listen to the dream –
However much it turns your heart to pulp.
Wealth and kingly power cannot save us from our fate.
Courage, brother, your time has not yet come
Your name was not recorded in the book.'

Enkidu lay unlistening, easing out of life.
Gilgamesh fell silent, bemused, frightened,
Remembering childhood prayers for help.
The dream was both as murky as a dust storm
And clear as dawnlight breaching the horizon.

★

For twelve more days Enkidu's body
Gripped his spirit like a drowning man
As he groaned and grimaced in resistance
To Irkalla's underworld of dust.
Then too sick to writhe he lay motionless
Like a lizard basking on a burning rock.
Finally, as if his last pouch of energy
Had ignited into words, he cried aloud:
'Can it come to this? That I, Enkidu,
Will not be killed in battle like a hero?
Am I cursed to slip away without glory
Like a woman or some toothless old man?'

Gilgamesh sat closer to his fading friend
Hoping to infect him with his life force.
Hour after hour beside the bier-like bed
He pictured random moments of their lives:
Ladling water from the broad Euphrates
Climbing up Mount Mashu's double peaks
Their adventures in the cedar forest
And every person flashed up in his thoughts:
The servants, ploughmen, women of the palace
And all the animals they hunted down –
The lions, leopards, stags and ibex –
Even the rivers, mountains and the woods,
Began to weep for one about to die.
Then Gilgamesh snapped from his reverie
Trapped his darting eyes within a glare
And cast it on his friend's relaxed face:
'What is this sleep that grips you, Enkidu?
Can you hear me? Has the darkness claimed you?
Enkidu, can you hear me? Can you hear me?'

★

His fingers touched a cheek; it felt like wax
And was stone-cold. He brushed Enkidu's eyes
To reassure himself they harboured sleep
But the lids had sealed the blind stare of death.
He touched his chest to feel the pumping heart
But heard his own heart pulsing in his head.
With a sheet he veiled his face, like a bride.
His masterful control then fell apart:
Sobs plunged up like vomit; he sank down heaving,
His flinching eye-slits radiated cracks,
His jaw unclenched a moan; he filled his lungs
And roared and roared like a lioness
Who's found her cubs bleeding from the throat.

Round and round the decomposing bed
Gilgamesh stalked, round and round, and round,
Stopped still; desperate to void his soul of grief
He pulled and tore his hair, ripped clothes, sank down
And curled up naked on the floor, grew silent
As his friend grew whiter every second.

All night he lay, his eyes astream with images.
At dawn he stirred his stiffened aching muscles
And saw his brother lying there, dead still.
Gilgamesh stared
And heard his voice cry from the tepid light:
'You shared my food, you rested on my bed
You were a prince, all Uruk paid you homage
You moved with grace, your limbs spoke power
We were two bodies of a single soul
You cannot die – I will not let you go.'

★

Still Enkidu did not move.

For seven days Gilgamesh wept and shivered
And all the while Enkidu grew less human
As Irkalla's mask tightened on his face.
Gazing at his brother's ash-grey cheeks
Gilgamesh felt his power drain away.
As his mind shut off the thought of death
A sudden rush of heat gushed from his heart
Forcing words out from his gluey lips:
'I will not let you go. There must be permanence.
I will make your flesh immortal.
Uruk's masons, goldsmiths and jewellers
Together will work the miracle of art
And give you such life no sleep, no death can touch.
Your body will be fashioned in beaten gold
Your chest inlaid with lapis lazuli;
By day when Shamash rises in his glory
Like a blazing beacon you will burn with life
And at night course silver like a waterfall.
Uruk and people from abroad will gape.
Scribes will stamp the stories of your deeds –
Humbaba's death in the cedar forest
The killing of the bull of heaven –
Their words will make you live forever
As long as men have breath to sing.'

As his words lingered in the fetid air
Gilgamesh, spent, gazed once more at Enkidu
And saw a worm peeping from his nostril
And knew the time was ripe to bed him in the earth.

Lazarus

*'This illness will not end in death; it has come
for the glory of God, to bring glory to the Son of God.'*
                                                John 11:4

It was near the feast of Passover
Some forty summers ago
That I died.
I have told this story far too often
But now I wish to tell it
For those who wish to hear
One last time.
I shall relate the truth as best I can.
But as the winter years approach
Memories stiffen in my bones.

Towards the end
There was the bed, the cool scent of Martha,
As the backs of her fingers brushed my face
Like petals on a branch,
Mary's undulating voice, drifting, subsiding,
The window's definition of blue light
Refining the sickness in my body,
Damped water drying on my forehead
And then nothing.

They took me to the cave
Where Mary and Martha were later laid to rest.
At some point, I cannot tell when –
For time had no sequence –
The dark began to blow away
I felt my self uncoiling

Unravelling into light
The sense of easily drifting from the flesh
Like an eagle shifting to a higher plane.
No words can approximate.
There was no up, no down
No before or after
All around the light was coarse
Grainy as a sand-drenched wind
But then the haze began to thin
And open up to purer light –
A brilliance seeped through my flesh
As if the sun without its heat
Was roaring out its radiance
And my skin and bones
Had melted into luminosity.
Awareness of my self dissolved
A gradual joy blossomed
Grew irrepressible, bursting, overflowing
Like wine glugging uncontrollably
From the throat of a jar knocked over.
Then the world appeared in sudden clarity
Landscapes reeling, cleansed, as after rain
The shocking focus
Of every crevice of every rock,
The greeny-yellow eye of a lizard
Every particle of dustlight freefalling
Bethany's deserted street
Chequered sharp with shade
A cockerel flashing the crimsons of its lobed comb
And in the distance, the walls of Jerusalem.

All the while
I saw my body in the cave
Could change perspective without willing –

As if by blinking I
Could look upward from my body
Or from above look down
As if body and fleshless floating self
Were joined by a thread of light.
Was this death or its threshold?
If it was death
Then I would say it is an expansion
A release from pressured flesh
A sense of being alive
No life can be prepared for.

The crowd shuffled up dust
As they ambled through the heat towards the cave
And I walked with them at the level of the ground
Among the knowing faces confident with doubt
Beside Mary and Martha
But could not touch their arms to comfort them.
Then I was above looking down.
Within the ragged throng
A circle of space had cleared around the Nazarene
Like the aura of the moon
And moved with him as he moved.
I tried to see his face
But could not – I was not ready
And there was too much grief,
Too much death on him.
If I had got too near his darkened soul
I knew I would have been obliterated.

Every single vibration shingled up towards me
Jolted the minute essence of whatever I was
As they moved away the stone.
I saw him look up to heaven

Not at me but through me
Then his outlandish cry —
The cry of one who has surrendered
The last hope of life —
Blew away the clarity of the world
Ushering in a misted vision
And the cry rolled up within itself
All the death cries
Of all the soldiers who had ever died
And all the wailings
Of every widow who had ever lived
Into its crescendo
Drawing me together
Drawing me down
An oozy heaviness drawing me down
As if my limbs were returning
And my organs were compacting into flesh
Then the cry erupted through me
As if the stone had been restraining
The massive tension of the sea
And now the waters of the oceans
Were presssured through the cave
Swallowing with foamy noise the life within me
Louder   louder   louder
Forcing me to re-inhabit flesh —
I felt my body move
A compulsion to escape coursed through me
And I realized
My will had returned.
A jagged blur of light in front
Pointed out the sole direction
As my body moved its weight of bones;
Then the light unpeeled
Into fiercer light, blinding, searing,

As if it were not light but visible heat.

Then the noise stopped.

Afterwards, for days,
People came from all around
To satisfy their longing
To see the freakish dead.
The rapture of disbelief
The heavy jostling, prodded questions,
Sneaked glances, darting touches.
Then the anger came:
The dog laid at my door
Its throat knifed away.
Then the sneers
Until I lived again
As an anecdote
The butt of jokes no longer hidden in my presence.
Finally, the death threats stopped.

And what of the young rabbi?
We loved him like a brother.
After that day, there were times
I hated him – as if he were a Roman.
For when he wept outside the cave
I knew it was because he had to sacrifice
A soul released from flesh
To make the crowd believe.
The people must have miracles
But miracles enrage...

In the Place of the Skull
Watchers slunk away before the end
Their eyes as bitter as the tips of nails.

Lightning ricked the hills
Unleashed rain spattered the gullies
And piercing the thunder
His cry stopped me breathing
For it was the cry I had heard before
And prayed I would never hear again.

'If a man believes in me,' he once said,
'It does not matter if he dies –
He shall come to life.
No one who is alive and has faith shall ever die.'
At first I had no use for faith.
I knew.
At night before the extinguishing of sleep
The fleshless buoyancy above the tomb
Would sometimes suddenly expand within
My head, unpetitioned,
Then fizzle out before my grasping mind.
So then I had recourse to words,
The joy of lighting up the eyes of listeners,
And the power.
But soon my practised answers
Encrusted my soul like rust
Day by day excluding air
Until my life became a rehearsal
For an event
Which had already happened.

Forty years on
I still ponder the events that day
My memory of them
And the words I have used to express them.
Something did happen
And if the words do not reflect the true reality

They describe a reality
I was unable to describe before.
Yet in trying to capture the mystery
I seem to fall farther from it.
Each time my story comes to life
Honed and hardened by conviction
I am resurrected
Into death by repetition.

Martha passed from this world
At the time of the great rebellion.
Mary followed soon after:
The roads lined with carrion bound to crosses
Ended her resistance.
For the rest of their lives
Their faces bore the radiance of his words
And he appeared to them
Soon after his death
As he appeared to others.
I never saw him again.
Perhaps my heart was too wrapped up in anger.

The land is deserted now.
Drought has reduced the river for the third year
The people have been scattered
Only the old, sick, lame and bedevilled
Only we remain
Nursing our enfeebled memories
Forgetting the sound of children
Comforting each other with tales of the past
Before the legions came to Bethany
Not daring to break new ground
And always at one remove from experience.

★

No one, he said, who is alive and has faith shall ever die.
If there is only one thing I would like to communicate
To those who would listen
And I say this as a warning
It is this: after I died
I never lived again.

The Road to Westport

'The car-boy presently yelled out "Reek, Reek!" with a shriek perfectly appalling. This howl was to signify that we were in sight of that famous conical mountain so named, and from which St Patrick, after inveigling thither all the venomous reptiles in Ireland, precipitated the whole noisome race into Clew Bay.'

W. M. THACKERAY

'Climb O holy men, to the top of the mountain which towers above and is higher than all the mountains to the west of the sun in order to bless the people of Ireland.'

The Book of Armagh

'We cannot go there by foot; for our feet only carry us everywhere in this world, from one country to another... Let all these things go and do not look.'

PLOTINUS

> The winding road from Westport sweeps
> Me out around its metalled curves.
> Far off white clouds unroll their bales
> Of cloth upon Croagh Patrick's head
> Then winds ease off its cowl and flood
> Its face with oceanic sunlight
> Until sheets of drizzle slither
> Across and mask the Reek again.
>
> At Murrisk and the mountain's base
> I start to crush the mushy path
> And broach the outer zone of vapours,
> Ascending at a steady rhythm
> My lungs blossom, my heart beats fast,

My face, relaxing into warmth,
Cools down from perforated mizzle.

The track leads me higher and deeper
Into a realm of formlessness.
Imperceptibly, my senses are erased.
Adrift in purgatorial smoke
I float between the sky and earth;
Constricted by the silence
My mind turns inward and receives
A stream of frayed anxieties,
Forgotten friends, unwanted guests,
Choice cameos of embarrassment
And yearns to lose its sense of self.

Anonymous flush-faced pilgrims
Bending forward heave on past me
Hands on hips or leaning on their staffs,
Inhibitions melting into bonhomie.
Ulster voices soften in the air
Their twanging accents fade away
As they slowly disappear.

Gradually the mist peels off
Its tracing paper from the world.
Sunlight tints the moss in parrot-green
Enamels rocks and pebbles
Gilds the bracken's dripping fronds.
From the earth soft plumes of vapour
Drift skyward like volcanic fumes.
To the north, the pores of steaming fields
Cleanse the soil, grass and wheat.
Clew Bay is sharpened into focus:
Shoals of smooth-backed basking islands

Prepare for the Atlantic ocean.
Silk threads of electrum light
Spin across the liquid corrugations
Of the aluminium sea.
Far off the mountains have collapsed
Into an avalanche of clouds.

Then, like an anaesthetic,
A sheet of mist blots out the world.
Within my shrunken planetarium
A shower of firefly memories
Streak across and die like shooting stars.

My feet slot back to a mindless trudge
And heave a body full of body.
Soon I am standing on a ridge
Where the distant views of north and south
Are simultaneously concealed.
The rain throws off its indecision
And spatters my hooded head.
Reaching a temporary pilgrim shelter
I huddle in the dead-lit dankness,
Look back and see KEVIN and BRIGID
Picked out in stones along a slope.
O God look down upon my name
And save me from obliteration.

The rain sieves itself to mizzle.
Again I set off brushing through
A mist of dewy spiders' webs
And finally approach the slope
Where the sharply angled path dissolves
Into a tidal wave of rocks.
Overtakers crunch on past me

The substance of their forms
Diminishing into wraiths.
Or from toneless ghostly shapes
Descending souls thicken into bodies.
Compulsively they say 'Not far now'
'Just ten minutes' 'You're nearly there'
And I feel briefly intimate
With each stranger passing by me.

The way is now so steep – standing straight
I stare directly at the sky.
Mist above me. Mist below me.
Mist by either side. I am alone
Apart from slowly shifting climbers
Who pick their way like tortoises
Through moisture-saturated air.
I pause, giddily look down
And – as from a banking aeroplane –
I see a port-hole in the clouds
An opened locket of the earth
Before the lid is shut again.

Back to the silhouettes and mist
The monotone of smoking rocks
I slip and scrabble over shale
But just as it appears I must be
Stepping through the clouds to heaven
The slope softens and the view
Is suddenly straight ahead.

I have arrived.

But all around a blindfold
Bandages the summit.

My eyes sift through the dense white layer
To glimpse the hidden land in vain.
I tell my soul to wait, and picture
The green-brown tartan of the fields,
The islands, stilled, as on a chart,
White-crinkled waves frilling the edges
Of the coast, the fingers of the sun
Stretching out behind a cloud
To sprinkle gold-leaf particles
On rows of shivering trees and hedges.

My will cannot enforce a hole.
In suspended animation
I watch the heads of pilgrims
Lead their bodies into view
Or slowly vanish from the rim
Trailing parachutes of mist.
I think of Patrick clanging his bell
To ward off swarms of demon birds
And drive away the pagan snakes
To banish death
And unite the tribes of Ireland
In a vision of the risen Christ.
Then without my willing it
Clouds drift apart like icebergs.
Beyond the snow-clumped fringes
As if looking through stained glass
I see a country beckon
Like distant mottled Canaan
Reflected in the dimming eyes
Of Moses on Mount Nebo.
Then the clouds reseal themselves
And memory flickers like an eyelid.

★

The way up and the way down
Are not the same.
With the first step from the summit
The sacred trance is at an end,
The goal is now the car park
And the road that winds to Westport.
Yet I grasp a fading selflessness
By giving heart to passing climbers:
'You're nearly there – just 10 minutes'
I say with genuine conviction
Though there is half an hour to go.

Walking sideways, braking with my knees,
I sense the Reek loom up behind me.
Half way down I stop, pause and talk
To a jaunty, peak-capped, smiling man;
Words tumble from his mobile lips –
No trace of his soul's suffering when
In one breath he turns from pleasantries
To his twins' death two months ago
And how his wife has sent him up
To kneel and say a prayer for them.

Farther down I reach the ridge
Where BRIGID and KEVIN luxuriate
In transient immortality
Waiting for their stones to be picked out.
On the final stretch, the pressured burn
Its turf-brown waters churned to foam
Invigorates my senses.
Each downward step allows fatigue
An extra foothold on my body.

Soon the car park's muted chromes
Revivify their colours
And the back of Patrick's statue
Brings me back to earth.

The road that leads to Westport
Shifts me from the misted peak
And trail of solitary climbers
To the land of crowded selves.
The Reek fragments in memory
But my inner eye can see the cloud
Roll slowly up the mountain's sides
Then gather and detach itself
To float above it like a canopy
Of snow, revealing on the summit
A white-cloaked congregation –
The blessed saints of Ireland,
Their necks and faces wine-lit
By the late sun's clarifying light:
Columkille and Columbanus
Finbarr and Ciaran of Clonmacnois,
Gall and Brendan the Voyager,
Aidan, Finnian of Clonard,
Brigid and Kevin of Glendalough
And those of the present
And those who are yet to come
All gathered on the mountain's peak
Facing the east, west, north and south
To bless the seamless country.

Then gradually the cloud descends
To veil the holy gathering

As the road takes me into Westport.

The Young Man of Galway's Lament

> *'As Mr Yeats puts it, the countryman's "dream has never been entangled by reality."'*
> LADY GREGORY, Poets and Dreamers, 1901

It was the first week of the falling year.
Your lips had touched the berries of the hedgerows
Leading from my home to the folded hills beyond;
The birds remembered the melodies
Your mouth would sweeten between reflective smiles;
Your absent breathing piled leaves against the wall
And raised the flames higher in the hearth.

You said once that before you would ever leave me
The Slievebloom Mountains would be worn away by wind
The Golden Vale of Tipperary would become as the Syrian
    desert
The sails of the Norseman would again unfurl the horizon
And snakes would dance a jig on Croagh Patrick's peak.

Your words deceived me, your eyes deepened my belief,
Your dimples were snares I fell headlong into
The pureness of your skin blinded me like snow
Your slender nape prolonged my innocence
And your kisses stole away the days of the week.

Winter brought you back to me.
Your sighs the north wind sent below my door
The stars shivered like the nerve tips of my spine
When the frosted gate-latch clinked and your footfall
Closed in on the top of my neck.

Every night the linen bedsheets tried to recall
The lolling heat and fragrance of your limbs.

You told me once I was the king of Munster
The king of Ulster, the king of Connacht
The king of Leinster, the high king of Tara
And that one thought of malice towards you
Would summon the feral armies of the Danes
The chain-mailed horses of the Norman knights
And the cold stare of the English men-at-arms.

The round towers of Ireland lie in ruin
Homesteads feed their stones to all the walls around them
The hermits have departed from the hills
The crows pick entrails from the broken roads
The rains boil the fields to slurry
But there never once took root in my breast
A single dark thought about you.

You played the goose with me, you dallied with me
You said the young men of Clare and Galway
At night when they lay with their women
All gazed on your face, your parted lips.
Your hair you said flashed the fire of a conquistador
Your cheekbones were fashioned in Córdoba
Your ankles were as fine as those of Queen Isabella.

When spring came it brought the memory of the spring
    before,
The morning we opened every door and window
And all the vapours smoking from the boglands
And all the vapours thinning down from clouds
Had suddenly vanished
And the colours of the hills and meadows were restored

In the gentle thaw of softened air.
There was rejoicing in the land
As if all the fiddle players from Cork to Donegal
Had opened windows to let their stringy music
Rise over trees and onward into river valleys
Over loughs and mountains into the breasts
Of every man, woman and child.

Summer will soon come upon the land.
It was the time you took yourself away
The time when wheat spilled over from the fields
The copper beeches flounced their heavy dresses
And the early sun blanched the stones of hilltop cairns.
Do you now dine at the table of a gentleman
And avert your eyes into a silver cup of wine?
Did you fall in with the tinkers of Leitrim or Fermanagh?
Or did you cross the ocean to the western isles
Where the salmon leap and the hazelnuts abound?

I will tell the sparrows to look for your blue dress
The winds will blow to me your spoor
The rivers will pass along your reflections
Churches will sound their bells if you should cross their
    thresholds;
At night the owls will spy the tracks and pathways
And the eyes of fish will break the surfaces of lakes.

You will hear my thoughts when I think of you at night.
When I read, your eyes will trace each word with mine
I will walk beside you as you walk
And rise with you from your bed.
I am before you, I am behind you
I am above you, I am below you
I am the rain that softens the ground you tread

The wind that parts the hair from your face
The sun that settles like a halo on your shoulders
And the moon that dims your shadow
Wherever like a shade you flit soundless
Over fairy mounds, through ancient woods
Beside the streams that gush from wounded mountains
Over bridges, past holy wells and crossroads
Through the height, width and depth of Ireland.

Praise for *A Vision of Comets*

'Mandalas, heavenly bodies, Greek mythology, temples and cathedrals give James Harpur's first collection a sense of the sacred running in parallel to the quotidian, and while the poems often reach into the exotic or esoteric, they are nevertheless accurately and cleanly made observances of a world the senses have access to'

POETRY IRELAND REVIEW

'Harpur's sensibility is attuned to love, time, myth, the "numinous" – the makings of poetry… Harpur has an imaginative wonder'

LONDON MAGAZINE

'Harpur's tunes are chiefly lyrical… the "welter of accumulated memories" is skilfully caught'

INDEPENDENT ON SUNDAY

'This is a fine and accomplished first collection… Harpur is just how I like poets – skilled, erudite, in love with language, and with proper humility'

STRIDE

New and Recent Poetry from Anvil

HEATHER BUCK
Psyche Unbound

TONY CONNOR
Metamorphic Adventures

PETER DALE
Edge to Edge
NEW AND SELECTED POEMS

DICK DAVIS
Touchwood

MICHAEL HAMBURGER
Collected Poems 1941–1994

ANTHONY HOWELL
First Time in Japan

PETER LEVI
Reed Music

THOMAS MCCARTHY
The Lost Province

E. A. MARKHAM
Misapprehensions

PETER RUSSELL
The Elegies of Quintilius

PHILIP SHERRARD
In the Sign of the Rainbow
SELECTED POEMS 1940–1989

RUTH SILCOCK
A Wonderful View of the Sea

A catalogue of our publications is available on request